WELL, LET'S JUST SEE HOW *the* DAY GOES

A Believer's Memoir of Finding Faith and Healing from Depression, Grief, PTSD, and Suicidal Ideations

RICK RODGERS

XULON PRESS

Xulon Press
555 Winderley Pl, Suite 225
Maitland, FL 32751
407.339.4217
www.xulonpress.com

xulon PRESS

© 2024 by Rick Rodgers

All rights reserved solely by the author. The author guarantees all contents are original and do not infringe upon the legal rights of any other person or work. No part of this book may be reproduced in any form without the permission of the author.

Due to the changing nature of the Internet, if there are any web addresses, links, or URLs included in this manuscript, these may have been altered and may no longer be accessible. The views and opinions shared in this book belong solely to the author and do not necessarily reflect those of the publisher. The publisher therefore disclaims responsibility for the views or opinions expressed within the work.

Unless otherwise indicated, Scripture quotations taken from the Holy Bible, New International Version (NIV). Copyright © 1973, 1978, 1984, 2011 by Biblica, Inc.™. Used by permission. All rights reserved.

Paperback ISBN-13: 978-1-66289-244-8
Ebook ISBN-13: 978-1-66289-245-5

I dedicate this book to my
personal support group

My bride and soulmate Lynda Palacz-Rodgers

My Children Caleb, Marriah,
Lyndsey, and Madison

My sister Catherine (Kay) Rodgers - Hayostek

My Pastor Dwight Seletzky

Preface

In my book, "Well, Let's Just See How the Day Goes." I attempt to share my story and help others face theirs.

I intend to reach out to others with hope and encouragement while helping them identify their support and healing throughout their life journey.

I desire to eradicate the stigma fellow believers have toward those who struggle with mental health issues.

Finally, I desire to partner with the church and provide support and resources to help foster wholeness and healing for those who struggle.

Rick Rodgers
Author, Certified Christian Mental Health and Life Coach

Foreword

Rick allows the reader to join in a complex yet fascinating world of survival, stabilization, healing, and eventually thriving as he seeks to serve God with his story and his journey as a Christian mental health coach, father, husband, and most importantly, servant of the Lord Jesus Christ.

As a Christian psychotherapist, I would suggest that this type of authentic glimpse into trauma, survival, and an eventual deepening awareness benefit all of us as we look at the way the past often influences our present life and behavior. Rick uses his true story and struggles to emphasize that we can change the narrative through faith and ultimately heal and improve our lives.

This is a wonderfully told, comprehensive guide to approaching mental health. The reader can also see an honest and raw look inside the brokenness of the human spirit through the lens of Rick as he battles depression and manages his mental health struggles. This is an honest view and ride that includes some excellent self-care tips and introductions to various types of therapies and approaches, and the critical factor is that it comes from a Christian perspective, with some excellent biblical references interwoven into a remarkable story.

What is beautiful and shocking about this story is that even the brutality of the experience that Rick has been through has bred the depth of Christ's love, expressed from one hurt believer to his fellow brothers and sisters. This is not a story that paints the usual rosy picture of all people of faith but rather an honest look at a type of abuse that can happen to any of God's children. Most importantly, though, it shows what one person can do with that experience and that pain to continue serving the Lord ultimately.

This book is a blessing to those who need encouragement, direction, and tips to get there.

Haven J. Ohly
Christian Psychotherapist

Table of Contents

Preface..vii

Foreword ix

Introduction 1

As the Story Goes............................7

Well, Let's Just See How the Day Goes 17

The Stories We Tell Ourselves and Others.... 27

Mental Struggles and the Church 37

What I Have Learned So Far 45

Ramblings of a Homeless Soul.............. 95

About the Author...........................101

Introduction

My name is Rick; I am known to many as a husband, a proud father of four fantastic young adult children, a cantankerous brother, and a sarcastic but cheerful friend. Most recently, I became a certified Christian Mental Health Coach. But the best descriptor that has brought me through my life thus far is that I am a child of God. This has brought me the most incredible peace and has helped me become who and what I am today. However, this wasn't always the case; it has been a process from my childhood to where I am now. There have been intense moments of conflicting thoughts and emotions. Throughout my life, I would often ask, "How can I know the love and acceptance of a Heavenly Father when I never knew my earthly father? What would be my reference point, or how would I recognize a nurturing, loving, and accepting love from God? Also, how could I get this unconditional love without such a reference point?" Growing up in a legalistic church also left me with an image of God as an angry old white-bearded man in heaven waiting to stick us with lightning bolts.

My journey started with doubt and confusion surrounding God's love for me. I often viewed God as absent, non-existent, and never present to help save me from my nightmares. If God loved me, why would He allow this or even have it as part of His plan? I had to learn how to accept the love of a Heavenly Father without ever having the reference point of an earthly Father. I want to share how I have walked through my complex PTSD, severe depression, and grief. I will also share with you how the enemy will try to destroy you through thoughts that are not true and set you up with abuse, pain, and fear. I remember the day God revealed to me that not having a reference to a sinful earthly father would be better for me because His love is pure. God's ability to heal all my broken pieces would be more effortless because there weren't negative preconceptions to contend with.

I have experienced a lot throughout my life, and as we know, God has a purpose for it all—even for destruction. Satan, however, comes to kill, steal, and destroy; his only goal is to keep us from our true calling. The confusion of my childhood and my attempts to process my adult life led me to attempt suicide three times. These experiences and the lessons I have learned through them have guided me and shaped how I currently employ these techniques as I move throughout my days. At first, the information I am about to share with you may appear impossible or too simple to apply to your situation, and I understand that. But remember that even though our head tells us we are the only ones who feel a certain way, we're not alone. There is a saying I like to use to remind myself: Everyone is fighting a battle that we may not know about.

One thing that has kept me going throughout my highs and lows is my faith in a sovereign and loving Father. Sure, there were days I would wonder if He even existed, but eventually my heart would return to 'its compass. I remember telling my pastor in an inpatient facility that maybe I was agnostic; with a gracious smile, he responded, "That's ok, Rick, God still believes in you." It's funny how when you are on a long journey, you are amazed when you look back and see how much territory you have covered. The greatest strength you will discover as a believer is your faith—a belief in something more significant and prominent than the pain and confusing thoughts you carry throughout your everyday existence. Who and what I am today can only be the work of a loving Father who has blessed me with my supportive family, friends, and one quirky pastor, whom I collectively call my support group. So, if you are reading my memoir, remember you are not alone; allow God to reveal who he has made you to be. When you are struggling and trying to make sense of life, let go of what you thought life should be, and let's just see how the day goes.

I am writing this book partly as a memoir of my journey and partly to share with you how I have grown and adapted to the symptoms I've experienced. My memoir is a historical account that helps me validate my experience to you, the reader. However, I must also share how I overcame and, hopefully, encourage you on your journey. If my life had a motto, it would be: Leave people better than how I found them. I own a Non-Profit called Loving Individuals Forming Transformations (L.I.F.T.). This motto is displayed there to convey our hearts towards two sectors of people: shelter-resistant homeless people and Christians who struggle with mental health issues. Our Christian mental health ministry is called Restoring Broken Vessels. As a Mental Health Coach, I work with individuals and in support groups to help

Well, Let's Just See How the Day Goes

Christians overcome or reduce the impact of depression, grief, and trauma.

While reading, you will hear my testimony and hopefully learn how to walk in your own freedom and recognize and control your mind, formed through Christ. The symptoms of grief and trauma can be debilitating, but by reading this book, you may learn and grow by immersing yourself in truth and practicing some strategies. However, remember that I am not suggesting you either avoid or embrace any medically proven treatment; I am simply sharing some organic and holistic supplements or alternatives to your current treatment. My goal is to integrate the truth of my faith in my journey with some proven therapeutic practices. Everyone is different, and each case must be handled using different approaches. Just keep in the back of your mind a saying I like to use to justify changes we must make to progress: You can't use an old key to open new doors. This book should never replace God's word, the Bible, but it is meant to supplement modern-day life and its challenges on the path leading us back to an amazing grace within a broken and fallen world.

As the Story Goes

Everyone has a story, and in this story there are the characters and, ultimately, a plot. It has been said that we never get to pick our family or the hand we have been dealt. However, we can change characters and how we interpret the plot at some point. This concept has become a significant journey of mine and is what has brought me through the healing journey I now walk through today.

I was born in Cleveland, Ohio, in 1965 to a single mom who spent the first three days of my newborn life debating whether she wanted to keep me or give me up for adoption. During those three days, my father walked in, gave my mother a hundred dollars, and told her he would keep in touch. His promise was never kept, and I never met him. My mother, who had been abused most of her life by other family members, was alone with my sister. Through poor choices and a narcissistic personality, she played both victim and perpetrator in our childhood abuse. On a visit to Cleveland, my grandmother did not like what she saw in my mother's abuse towards us, and she decided to take my sister back home to Pennsylvania to live with her, leaving me behind to face my mother's fury. The abuse she gave me and allowed others to do to me covered all areas and continued throughout my childhood. Looking back now, I can identify these simple truths as the reasons for her abuse towards me. It was her way of being afraid, living out learned behaviors, and getting back at the men who abused her.

Eventually, when I was around six years old, my mom could not afford to live in Cleveland anymore, and we moved back to her childhood home in Pennsylvania. She had no place to live except with her mother, and my sister and I were reunited. Part of me felt hopeful because I was with a sister who was five years older and tried to protect me. I was also reunited with my other cousins, one of which was my cousin Greg, who became like a brother to me. We went on so many adventures together with our imaginations. Because we were both born in April, his birthday being the second and mine the thirtieth, we would always share a joint party on his birthday, and mine was never celebrated. Eventually, my Aunt Helen, who lived in Ohio, wanted her son to move to Cleveland when we were both in the fourth grade.

Well, Let's Just See How the Day Goes

That was the first loss I could ever remember having as a young boy, the first time I felt what I would later know as grief.

I remember my mother always saying, "You are just like your father, and I wish you were never born." The physical beatings were sometimes severe and fueled mainly by her frustrations as a single, deserted mother. The other abuses I experienced, whether directly from her or from others, included sexual, mental, emotional, and spiritual. Unlike the prevailing medical professional opinion, I believe that mental and emotional are two different types of abuse. Emotional abuse is when someone tries to control your emotional reaction. My mother would become very violent with me, and the more I would scream or cry, the more she would threaten me; she would say, "If you don't stop crying, I will give you something to cry about!" The beatings would become worse and even included banging my head against the wall. I was responding to the physical pain, which is normal, but she tried to control my emotional response. In addition, she would punch me in the stomach, causing me to lose my breath. These beatings often happened when she fought with others or had a bad day at work. Usually, on Sunday nights, the family would get together to watch WWF Wrestling, and our mother would get angry. At this point, she would take me into the nearest bedroom next to the living room and start beating me. The noises she would make while venting her frustrations on me caused the family to roar with laughter. The more they would laugh, the more she would abuse me. Looking back on it today, I believe my mom loved the attention she was receiving from the family that had been abusive to her growing up.

During my life, I was also passed around to other abusive family members. When I was three, my mother gave me to my aunt and her pedophile husband who abused his three stepchildren. He was a retired police officer, full of rage, and had multiple guns that he would hold up to our heads. At a young age, I learned how to fear for my life when I was locked up in a dark attic and suffered being sexually abused. Since I was the youngest child, my aunt would try to protect me, but her two sons resented that she wanted to shelter me and not her own, which led them to abuse me even worse. Later in life, I learned that my female cousin became pregnant at the hands of her stepfather, and she was made to raise her daughter. My cousin's abuse and rape caused her to overdose on heroin later.

Eventually, I returned home to my mother, where the abuse would continue and intensify, and I was exposed to other forms of abuse. The spiritual abuse happened to me both in the home and within the church. This form of abuse was by far the scariest because it felt permanent, and there would be nothing I could do about it. Growing up in a small town can be a good thing, but for me, it was a place where everyone knew everyone's business. So, everyone knew it was my final judgment when my religious grandmother said I was possessed and going to hell because I was conceived out of wedlock. In my earlier years, I was raised to believe that I was weird, mental, gay, and would never amount to much of anything. I lived in abuse, shame, and fear in my earlier years. I was entirely stripped of hope, love, and confidence, and the only faith I knew was grounded in legalism and eternal damnation.

My mother had four sisters; Aunt Janet married a pedophile, Aunt Arbutus lived next door to Grandma, Aunt Helen resided in Cleveland, and my Aunt Sharon was the meanest to all her nieces and nephews. One day, my Aunt Sharon told my mother, "Catherine, you better be careful because someday your son will strike back at you." That day came when

I was fourteen. Following the normal dragging me to the room where my abuse often occurred, the beating started, and something snapped inside me. With my right hand, I pushed her off me, and she flew into the wall. She started crying and said, "Look what you did to me; how could you?" I felt full of shame and guilt, and I started crying. There, she knew she had total control and power over me.

In the summer of 1980, when I was fifteen, we went to Cleveland to visit my Aunt Helen and cousin Greg. While on our visit, my cousin asked why I was bruised. I told him what was going on back home. I told him how it got worse when I stood up to her, and I feared what I could have done to her. Greg got so mad and went and told his mother. Greg returned later to ask me if I wanted to move to Cleveland to live with him and his mom, and I said yes. All I could feel was freedom, that I had been rescued. My feeling when my mom agreed was incredible; I would no longer live fearing being abused, and my life would be better.

Little did I know that my new life would only begin an internal struggle that would replace the external pain. At age eighteen, I made my first suicide attempt by overdosing. Throughout my teenage years and early twenties, I used drugs and alcohol to deaden my pain. I aimed to die by age thirty, so I lived on the edge. When I turned nineteen, I got my first real job as a server in a downtown tenth-floor restaurant. There, I met celebrities and served at exclusive events. My life felt so complete that all my years of abuse washed away as I lived vicariously through prestigious and influential people. My life was filled with intervals of hope and disappointment; I walked away from my faith in the God of my childhood. I lived my life on my terms, never knowing I was living out the prophecy that my grandmother spoke over my life.

Then I woke up one day, worn out from the parties, late-night bar hopping, and long work days. My life was getting worse as I discovered that living on my terms didn't produce the results I had hoped for. Spending several hours and days taking inventory of my life, I remembered some of the good times I had as a child in Sunday school. My sister, who was finishing up Bible school in Pennsylvania, must have been praying for me. So, I returned to church around the age of twenty-two and rededicated my life to Christ. I moved out of my aunt's house and rented a small house with a guy I had met at church. I started dating the pastor's daughter, and eventually my roommate started dating a girl, and we would always double date.

After a few months, something began to shift in this four-person relationship. My roommate's girlfriend and I remained faithful to our partners, but my girlfriend and roommate were sneaking around. The day came when my roommate broke up with his girlfriend, and it became apparent that I had lost my girlfriend and a roommate. Soon after my roommate moved out, I started receiving calls from my roommate's ex-girlfriend. We continued with the friendship, which was initially rooted in sorrow stories.

Then something unique happened; it came together, and my life was about to become complete. As our relationship grew, we found ourselves falling in love. I started noticing a young woman who wasn't like all the female influences I had experienced in my childhood. She was gentle, sweet, warm, and nurturing to a broken, wayward soul; she made every day seem new and exciting. But it would take two rejections and three proposals to have her hand in marriage finally. Why the rejections, you ask? Because even though she saw the potential in me, she also saw the uncertainty, the fear, and the broken boy. But God knew she would be the one to see me and love me, and he would use her to help heal me eventually. We were married in the fall of 1991 in front of friends, family, and those who said we would never succeed. My ex-girlfriend and ex-roommate, who had married a few months earlier, even made it clear that, unlike ours, their marriage was ordained by God. I must warn you: be very careful what you say to others. God is all-knowing. He sees into the future; in my case, He knew what I would need around me to become who I am today. In thirty-two years of marriage, my wife and I have often remarked how our lives would have been so different if we had married our exes; she would sometimes say, "You know your ex would have never stayed with you." As always, my wife was right; my ex would have left at the first sign of depression or suicide attempt.

The first three years of our married life were hard. I now look back and laugh, stating, "My wife broke me." When we were first married, I had no idea I had an anger problem, and I would always raise my voice to intimidate. I never called her names, but I would use stern words. The problem was that she would not yell back or participate in my rage. I would scream, and she would not say anything. When questioned if she would argue back, her response to me would be, "NO!" I found it hard to argue alone, and eventually my behavior changed. My anger went dormant and internal, but it did not go away. Because I did not deal with it through counseling or treatment, it festered within. It is essential to realize that "anger" is a displaced emotion, and it is attached to an underlying root. This root for me was depression, PTSD, and grief. We will talk later about how not addressing issues can cause them to manifest in different ways, but for now, I will say that it can affect relationships. However, as I mentioned in the introduction, allowing God and your support group into your darkest moments to speak truth, hope, and healing is essential. I believe with my whole heart that this has been my saving grace and what has helped me heal the most from a troubled beginning. I pray that reading this book will help illuminate your heart and that my story will resonate with you about the pain and the journey but also, ultimately, about the hope that awaits.

Well, Let's Just See How the Day Goes

I was initially diagnosed with severe depression, and as my doctor visits continued, it appeared that new diagnoses were often added to my medical history. One of my diagnoses that was added at some point was Bipolar. When I discovered this diagnosis, I questioned how we came to this conclusion. The doctor responded, "Well, you told us that when you were a teenager, you would spend days being up and running around, followed by days of sleeping." I laughed and responded, "Really, we called it using speed back then." I asked the doctor if he would change my diagnosis and remove the medication from my ever-growing list. He replied, "No!" At one point, I was on eight medications and a clinical medical diagnosis of "treatment-resistant depression." For this reason, I was always on various medicines, constantly adding and changing prescriptions.

I was seeing a physician's assistant at the time who enjoyed prescribing medications. On one office visit, I asked if we would ever sit with a psychiatrist and review my case. He was surprised that I would want a review and responded with, "Why? Your case isn't that serious." I continued with a question: "Why am I on so many medications if my case isn't so serious?" A question that is probably dumbfounding him to this day. Looking back, I believe the massive amounts of drugs I was taking caused problems with my suicidal ideations. Both my wife and pastor, two key people in my support group, always would question my treatment plan. It is always a best practice to be proactive and ask about your medical care and treatment. Because, in my case, a prescription cocktail like mine also produced suicidal ideations. Always remember that medical professionals only practice medicine, and medical studies constantly change. My best advice to anyone taking medication is to listen to your body, always looking for how it makes you feel. Question yourself and see if there are things you can do without a prescription to produce the same, if not better, results. I hope to convey that to you through my writing of this book.

Well, Let's Just See How the Day Goes

A person who suffers from PTSD and depression, like everyone else, has choices they must make on any given day. These decisions can often become skewed because of internal thoughts, emotions, and how we perceive our environment. We tend to make these decisions from points and places of previous hurt and abuse. We rationalize that it is best to avoid life and reduce the risk of triggers from dark places we have previously experienced. The best way I would explain this concept would be to reference an old saying. I have always heard it said, "It is better to lose in love than never to love at all." I would challenge that statement and with a simple but thought-provoking rebuttal: why? Why would I allow myself the pain of getting close to something that would hurt me? What is the purpose of taking risks, falling, and reinjuring a sore? There were times, specifically earlier in my married life, when I would question whether my wife loved me. Would I even know the thrill if I never knew what it was like to drive a car, experience a carnival, or ride a raging river? If I never knew love or experienced it, would I know what I was missing? In other words, I can't miss something I never experienced.

Most mornings, while everyone else started their day, I struggled deeply in my depression to get dressed and face the outside world. Thoughts of nothing good happening and of how remaining inside would be safer in the long run would flood over my emotions. Why would I want to face challenges when staying in my comfort zone was safer? When my depression was high, I would isolate myself, and if I didn't have to engage with the world, I didn't. I would make plans with family or friends, and when the time would come, so did the excuses. Because I wanted to please others, I feared hurting them by exposing myself in my depression. The classic Eeyore syndrome was not wanting to bring others into my depression. Family and friends would call during these seasons, and I couldn't find the strength to answer. I would sleep a lot, go days without showering, and my wife would remind me how many days I had been wearing the same tee shirt and sweatpants. My energy and drive would worsen because I was always going, doing, and accomplishing things only when my medication worked. The problem with thinking this way is that nothing gets accomplished, and the depression gets deeper as the day goes on. One day, around ten a.m., I returned to bed with the blanket over my head. Suddenly, I realized that this bed had become my coffin.

I will be the first to tell you that nothing is ever accomplished, solved, or rewarded by living out the practice I just described. I understand the emotions and lack of energy behind depression, the fear of unexpected triggers that loom outside your comfort zone, the internal struggle it takes when you inventory where you are currently and where life requires you to be. Just having to explain to others what you are feeling in the moment can sometimes take the very life out of you. The dilemma I always faced was how to answer the simple question, "How are you?" More often than not, I would ignore it and deflect it with another question. These are social coping skills; we feel we are protecting ourselves by deploying them. However, we are not protecting ourselves by hiding from those who love and care for us. By deflecting, we push others away that we love the most, and they cannot understand why we push them away. PTSD, depression, and grief hurt us and those around us. Even though we might not want others around, they still want to be around us, and it was in this area that I realized I was being selfish and withholding myself from those who did find me lovable.

Cognitive Behavioral Therapy

One of the best therapies I have ever embraced is Cognitive Behavioral Therapy (CBT). This training has helped me overcome negative self-talk, isolation, and wrong interpretations of others' intentions. Before learning these skills, I would live like a victim, finding fault and waiting for the worst to happen in any given situation. I struggled with relationships, getting close to others, and sharing deeply personal matters. If I did share too much, my concern would linger about how it might be used against me. CBT is used in most inpatient settings for patients with mental health issues; it is a systematic approach to help identify and minimize the impact of negative emotions and behaviors. I have used these concepts with family, friends, and people I help coach.

Cognitive Behavioral Therapy helps condition the mind by turning a negative thought into a positive one, thus preventing a downward spiral mindset. I was introduced to it while in a treatment center. One of the techniques I learned there was called "self-talk." When a person is depressed, having a panic attack, or experiencing a trigger from PTSD, their mind tries to process and make sense of what is happening.

Pulling your past experiences and emotions into the future is confusing, and when a trigger happens and you're caught off guard, that is where the internal conflict takes hold. I would try to apply the exact solutions or copy skills from my past to escape the current perceived threat. The problem arises when the present situations are not as intense. We can use an adult solution, but our child and victim minds try to solve the threat. We tend to lean into a negative frame of mind, so our self-talk is negative. What is that self-talk saying, and what can we do about that self-talk? Now, this is where this concept takes practice. We must increase our ability to realize what is happening and learn how to change the thought process track. It took a lot for me to work through this, and thankfully I had my pastor cheering me on, reminding me to have grace for myself. I needed to determine what approach I would need and the positive self-talk verbiage to begin another CBT skill called "Opposite Action."

Pulling this together would go something like this: When I was invited somewhere, all these thoughts of what could or might happen would overwhelm me, and I would find myself making excuses to back out. I would need to employ self-talk that would tell me why what I was thinking was wrong and how I would need to try; the opposite action would be the technique of going through with the plan. Reframing, another CBT skill, would help me re-process negative thoughts into positive realities. Instead of thinking, "They will notice my depression and critique my actions," I would start by reframing the event in a positive light by employing self-talk so that I could be present and engaged. That in turn, would lead me to do the opposite of just staying away from others and believing my self-perceived thoughts. On the outside, friends saw someone who was quirky, social, and somewhat entertaining, but inside, I would try to regulate how much to do and speak. I did this to mask my internal world. Being alone in a crowded room or hearing the silence in a room full of conversation was, and at times still is, how I experienced most social gatherings.

Another CBT technique I had to implement is "self-care"; this is where you do things for yourself that help you feel better about yourself. Ever notice when you have been sick with the flu, and you're lying around trying to get better, and the day comes when you finally feel a little better? Showering, putting on clean clothes, and putting new sheets on the bed all

Well, Let's Just See How the Day Goes

help you feel good and on the road to recovery. This skill helped me turn the corner and start my mind off each day with positive and motivating ideas, leading to challenging myself with the phrase, "Well, let's just see how the day goes." This isn't just positive but adventurous, and it was the only thing that would pull me out of my coffin. At first, this may be hard to embrace, but by taking small baby steps and having grace for yourself when you don't make the next step, you will be okay.

As a believer, I was never alone in this process because I remember praying and asking my Father to help me on those days that I did fall short. I invited God, through the Holy Spirit, to meet me where I was, to be my strength. One of my favorite verses is in Galatians 2:20, where Paul talks about how he lives not through his own power but through Christ living inside him. Not I, but through Christ in me. God, I can't, but I know You can! This scripture refers more to our sinful nature and Christ working in us for a new life, but I believe this can apply to anything that hinders or interferes with our walk with Christ. In our journey to normalize all that has been done to us, it is essential to remember that we all have our unique relationship with God. Since everyone has their own story, as the word says, we must all work out our salvation. Here, our relationship with God will look different to others; though the core Gospel is the same for all, my personal issues will be different from others and, thus, how God interacts with and through me may be different from how he works with others. This means my story with His healing will not always be from the textbook of others' journeys; we are uniquely formed, and God has different lesson plans.

The Stories We Tell Ourselves and Others

A friend once told me, "It's not the beginning of the story that matters but the end." Everyone has a story; we are simply narrators, and our Heavenly Father is the author. We learned in elementary school that every storyline must have a plot, conflict, and, most importantly, the ending. Every chapter builds upon the previous one; some choose to move toward our purpose or action, and others never do. In my life, I have had to keep this mindset. What story am I showing others? What narrative am I displaying, and how does that align with what God has created me to be? In the mind of a person who has suffered from early childhood trauma, life is complex with confusing mixed messages. The triggers we experience help validate the internal stories and support the emotions we experienced in the past. I create negative thoughts whenever someone says we need to talk. My mind seems to receive those words as a threat.

Someone once explained that to me as waiting for the other shoe to drop; I always expected the worst. Sensing the threat of danger has been rooted in me since childhood. My friend, I am here to tell you that this thinking can be mentally exhausting. This happens because we hang onto words, predicting what will be said and that it will be in anger when they're presented. If this is in the workforce, we plan our exit strategy and remove pictures from the wall, setting things back to how they were before we arrived, as if we never existed. Throughout my life, starting at a young age, I would remove friends and, at times, even family from my life to avoid potential rejection. I was my own worst enemy; I didn't need people to hurt me. As the saying goes, hold my beer!

Throughout my battles with PTSD and depression, I have often shifted focus from reality to feelings. However, in the last few years, I have learned that emotions must be managed and controlled so they do not skew my reality. This is where the concept of the stories we tell ourselves has helped me rise above the emotional struggles because I often found myself in bondage to these stories. I was talking to myself and others from a place of negative narratives. The little boy is locked in the attic, afraid and victimized.

Like a movie reel inside, my mind repeatedly rewired and played out the same old scene. I saw myself as, and presented the hidden message of being, damaged goods, not worthy of love and happiness. This destructive monster image I created of myself led me to believe that something wrong with me caused the abuse and warranted everything ever done to me. I did not deserve a loving wife, wonderful children, or a sister who would stand up for me, even in my darkest times. But they loved me more than the internal and external image I saw within myself. My pastor was like a mirror to me, constantly reflecting biblical truth and a father's steadfast love for me. He wasn't like the pastors I knew growing up; he operated in mercy and grace. Even in our relationship, I would beg him to be demanding of me, condemning and judgmental towards me. Like that little boy, I needed a reference point to justify the curses spoken over me as a child. God knew what I needed and what it would take to get me to where I am today. My support group could not always understand my past, but they saw my potential. Somehow, through the struggles, I still believed, hoped, and wanted God to heal me.

If we don't manage our emotions and skewed views of reality, we can hurt ourselves and those we love. When we operate out of a false reality, we shift into victim mode, where everyone is a potential perpetrator, whether they know it or not. This will divide us from those who love us and are invested in a deep and meaningful relationship with us. When we employ this victim approach, it will affect newer relationships as well. Just like making a significant purchase, people, upon first meeting us, often evaluate whether a friendship is worth the investment. When we tell our stories, we need to remember our audience and how they might interpret the messages sent and received. Remember that I am not advocating that we suppress or downplay our experiences, but not everyone we meet can benefit from our experiences. In other words, "Never bleed on those that never cut you." In my struggles thriving on false narratives and runaway emotions, I would get mad at everyone and withdraw. I would give them the same silent treatment my grandmother gave me as punishment, grounded in shame and disappointment.

There are four distinct types in the study and assessment of "attachment styles". These types reflect how we are with others within any given relationship. For example, I have a disassociated style because of how I was raised. This type would tell others, "I hate you, don't leave me." This conflicting message is created from fear, danger, and a desperate need to be protected by the one abusing us. Most of my abuse came from a mother who entangled abuse and nurturing. Because she suffered abuse from childhood, she did not know how to be a mother. As an adult, as I mentioned earlier, she would do anything for attention; if her mother found it funny for her to abuse me, that was all the motivation she needed. You can learn more about the four attachment styles by taking an assessment online. Knowing how I tend to be in relationships has helped me improve my relationship with others and refocus on healthier, more meaningful bonds.

What is truth? Finding this answer is a prevalent, historical, and biblical quest that has followed us since the beginning of time. There are segments of reality that we know to be true, which we then classify as truth. For example, we know gravity holds us down, so this is true! We also know that playing with fire can burn us. It has also been proven that if you don't try, you will never learn or, at times, succeed. So where do those stories we tell ourselves fit in? What is the basis of these stories? A lot depends on our frame of mind when we tell them. Negative self-talk will say, "I will never," which we use as an excuse, a standard narrative in our stories, to justify our failures before they happen. Then we follow up with words like "can't" or "won't," which I have always called absolutes. I have lost out on many potentially good experiences or opportunities using these absolutes. I remember the sibling challenge my sister and I once held when we didn't want to make our mother a grandparent. In our younger twenties, we would say, "I won't get married, or if I do, I won't have children." Because of our childhood, the abuse and fight for survival kept us frozen from living life to the fullest. Our mother used to say to us growing up, "The way you treat me, your kids are going to treat you ten times worse." It wasn't that we were bad children, but our mother didn't know how to be a single parent. Thank God we never held onto those absolutes. They weren't really the truth. Today, my sister is married with three wonderful children, and my life has become complete by having my son and three amazing daughters. My sister and I would have never known the love of our spouses that God would use to help heal us.

As someone who manages day-to-day interactions with others, the potential for triggers is always in my rearview mirror. Will the attack come from the words or actions of co-workers, friends, or even family in my environment? We never really know how something might trigger a memory, the magnitude of that trigger, or its impact. But we must control it and use whatever tool or resource we can to manage it before it affects those around us. Remember, this is our condition; we cannot expect others to tap dance around us, always being on guard for our reactions. As I have grown into the person I have become, I have had to step back and reject knee-jerk reactions or emotional outbursts. I remind myself that everyone is fighting some battle internally or might just be having a bad day. Also, we need to remind ourselves of how we interpret the current situation by taking inventory of experiences from our past. What potential influences are they playing in these everyday situations? How would others even know about our history, or how might it affect us? Even if what we are experiencing results from an intentional attack, how can we minimize how it impacts us? We need to separate our childhood trauma and all of what we experienced and not let it control how we interpret our current situations and surroundings. My frustration with my adult conflicts can be exacerbated because I am trying to incorporate my inability to understand or solve my childhood threats.

My mother passed away at the age of eighty in 2021. I visited her at her bedside days before she passed away; as she faded in and out, I asked her to forgive me for being a difficult child. She opened her eyes, looked at me, and said, "You were just a child; what did you know?" I was expecting an apology from her, to be honest. How could she not take any responsibility for the physical, sexual, mental, emotional, or spiritual abuse I had experienced? I can still remember leaving that nursing home in shock and eyes filled with tears. She, like all my other abusers, died without ever saying they were sorry. This troubled me for weeks after she passed away; I couldn't attend her funeral because, deep inside, I was hurt and angry and unwilling to put all the past behind me and move on.

One night, as I prayed for God to heal me of this brokenness, I heard a still, gentle voice saying, "She could only walk in the light she was given." In my trauma, I had to realize a few simple truths. First, my abusers can't hurt me anymore. Second, they, at one point, were also abused, and that was the only way they could cope. That what happened to me was my fault was the story I had been telling myself repeatedly, a little boy in grown-up clothes, a victim of my past. That narrative never works. And it prevents healthy growth and healing, leaving behind a destructive path of hurting others, especially those God has given us to love and nurture. The thought process by which I left that story behind might not be a textbook way of dealing with traumatic childhood events, but it is what helped me. Forgiving never means you forget, but you release them from what they did to you. Hurt people, hurt people. Jesus taught us how to walk in mercy towards others, and forgiveness was my act of mercy. This commandment Jesus taught has been instrumental in my healing because it put me into a humble understanding with my abusers. So, in summation, we are a story that God creates, and we live and respond within this story; we become the narrators. Allow God the opportunity to write the story based on what He intended. Stop taking the pen from Him.

Mental Struggles and the Church

A couple of years ago, I was working out at our local gym and minding my business. This should be a clue: stories that start with someone minding their own business never really turn out well. As I broke a sweat on the cardio equipment, praying and reading scripture on my phone, a gentle, empowering internal voice spoke. Mentally, I heard, "You, like Moses, will lead your people." My first question was, as you might have guessed, "What people?" Then, just like a file cabinet opening, I saw myself, the struggles, and the constant battle between my faith, the Christian community, and my continuous mental health struggles. I saw myself as the little boy struggling within a legalistic church which, though it sometimes acted as a refuge from the abuse at home, was full of heavily imposed demands from the pulpit. We were conditioned to live in fear, constantly questioning when and how God would punish our every move—the constant confusion between mental struggles, judgment, and God's love for us. I remember, at a young age, equating pain with love. It was always instilled in me that I was being punished because I was born a bastard and that God was not pleased with me. How could a loving God stand by and watch my abuse within the church and at home? Looking back now, I can see how the devil tried to destroy the very spirit and soul within me. How could God use me like He did with Moses? What could I offer "my people?" I was damaged goods, working very hard to bury the anger and pain from my past. Sure, I may not have killed a fellow Egyptian as Moses did, but I did leave a path of destruction.

I was once described by a Christian counselor in our church, a family friend and mentor, as a "complex individual." I respected his heart but felt isolated, different, and alone through the emotional turmoil brought on by my depression, grief, and PTSD. Sure, I believed that God loved me and that I was, after all, His child, but I felt that I was somehow not normal enough to proclaim His faithfulness. Attending church and seeing happy people living affluent and fulfilled lives didn't help my feeling of failure. Feeling different in the crowd does not promote inclusion;

it reminds us of how diverse, and at times peculiar, we appear to others. The ugly duckling story ends well; however, we see the conflict amid the story. The church was designed to be a hospital for those physically and spiritually sick, but no one ever mentioned being mentally or emotionally ill. Churches across the nation, throughout the years, have focused on God's unique ability to transform societal behaviors, but mental issues have remained silenced and often ignored. Catchy phrases like "Brother, you just got to cast down those feelings and trust God for your healing" have become the worst armchair counseling attempt I have ever heard. I don't want to appear disgruntled, and I will admit my pastor was very helpful and instrumental in my earlier treatment strategies and hospitalizations from the beginning. As a body of believers, though, the church must come alongside the widow suffering from grief and the teenager battling depression, which requires more than just Christian-style TED talks.

My journey has been long and sometimes very complicated, but like anything else, it is a process. It has been a series of sprints in an ongoing marathon. Like it was for Moses, it has been a constant desert journey, moving in circles, but eventually, with God's guidance, he led his people through. My hope in writing this is that you will see a few key points. First, you are not alone; there is hope and healing, but only with steps forward and backward. If you can really hear even just that one thing, this will confirm the guidance I received at my local gym while minding my own business.

As one can guess, most of my battles with mental health issues stemmed from my childhood experiences. My heart loved the ideas and concepts of a nurturing Heavenly Father, but my head struggled with the idea of a loving Father allowing pain and suffering in my world. As I mentioned, the church wasn't always a haven for me growing up, and elders weren't always godly men acting according to their biblical calling. The pulpit was, at times, a place of judgment and damnation laden with inconsistent order. My family was skeptical of most churches' direction, resulting in massive church hopping. This behavior produced uncertainty, trust issues, and contention among family members. Reactions from churches upon our leaving and the constant striving eventually caused many of my family members to fall away from the faith. As a result, my grandmother became very legalistic and angry, resented organized

Well, Let's Just See How the Day Goes

religion, and often dismissed teachings that didn't fit her narrative. My mother left her faith, leading her to increased mental health issues. She replaced her faith with the need to work, earn, and buy things to fill a void. When I was twelve, my mother had her first mental collapse, which resulted in her becoming hysterical and out of control. I came home from school and found her on the edge of the couch crying and mumbling, "They are coming to get me." This was all triggered by my mother's lack of organizational skills and losing an overdue bill. Where was the church, the believers we would have fellowshipped with previously? The people that did come around acted in proper Job's friends-like fashion. Job's friends started with seven days of weeping alongside Job, but right after those days, attitudes changed. Around chapter four, they started expressing personal opinions and potential causes for Job's pain and suffering, all of which put the blame on Job himself. This was my earliest view of faith and the constant internal struggle within the church for me.

As I previously mentioned, my experience with the church and its leaders wasn't the best in my younger years. Trusting in man or an establishment run by sinful people in a fallen world isn't easy. People often say it is a miracle that I want anything to do with God or His church. Maybe that is why when I came to Cleveland, I avoided church and fell away myself; after all, I was raised on how to perform before an angry God and abused in the process. The Bible says the fathers' sins are generational and continue to affect us. Leaving the church wasn't my problem; abandoning my faith in God is what led to a self-destructive lifestyle. This lifestyle put me in several dire circumstances that could have ended very badly, even in my death. I was in a mental hospital by age eighteen, questioning how I got there.

Community is essential, and there is safety in the abundance of counselors, but without a relationship with God, it is useless. We all know of Christians in name only who love the fellowship with others but seriously lack the relationship with Christ that calls us into obedience and holiness. On my map, I could honestly say I was here! There was no reference point for a father figure in my life, so once again I was struggling and blaming God for abandoning me when I was the one who walked away. It never dawned on me until years later that I had lived my life and the formed its narrative to create the God I thought I wanted or deserved. I wanted to live life on my terms and blame God when it went wrong. Can you imagine how employing that same concept with our family would play out? As my father, God had allowed me to suffer greatly, so I assumed He was absent, and because of this, I decided to do it my way. This was like the Israelites waiting on Moses while he was up on the mountain, out of sight and out of mind: I know, let's do it our way!

It took years and me becoming a father to my children for me to fully understand a father's heart and his love. Realizing our human nature and how we love imperfectly changed my views on God, man, and the church. This understanding led me to walk out my healing and build my faith. Don't get me wrong, like my faith, I am still walking out my recovery and will probably continue until I am called home. I learn and see more of God's grace daily as He reveals Himself to me. It is at that moment when I feel my Father's unconditional love that my healing will overcome my brokenness. You might think the church should be flawless, with Christ as the head, but the flawlessness is gone as soon as we walk into it with our scars and wounds. But like Moses, I will continue to lead myself and others on this journey through the desert wilderness till we reach the Promised Land.

Throughout my walk in the faith, I have encountered some very rigid Christians. Are you aware of the ones I am talking about? They are the ones that make you feel evil or less spiritual because you haven't trusted Jesus enough, and they seem to equate 1 Peter 5:7 with a remedy. "Brother," they say, "Let Jesus give you joy, pray more, and read your Bible. You'll be fine." I am not sure if they think they are helping or hurting those of us who struggle. You need to be reminded that Jesus felt every human emotion, including depression; Jesus got tired, weak, and even wept at times. Jesus did not scold people with these issues but ministered to them, just like His Father ministered to Elijah in the wilderness. So as saints, we imitate Christ and do the same. We can remind others what Jesus said in John 16:33, "In this world, you will have tribulations, but take courage: I have overcome." During tribulations, we will get depressed, become discouraged, and even shed a tear. I stand in my faith, realizing my humanity within a fallen world, knowing that Christ died to save me and that He will return and restore me. However, I have also learned that the church is the bride of Christ, and even though we aren't perfect, we need to have grace for His bride.

What I Have Learned So Far

In our church, I saw this sign that said "Give, Serve, Grow," and it spoke to me like nothing else I had ever seen before. I learned early in my recovery from depression and grief that serving helped me escape my internal world. Also, my experience has been that we grow when we give back or serve others. So, in writing my memoir of who, what, and where I have been, I give back to you, the reader, in hopes of helping you in your walk. I desire that as you read my story and see my constant struggle to be all that God created me for, it would give you hope and encouragement to do the same. Remember, this is a journey towards your destination; triumphs will be mixed with days of defeat. Take courage and run that race, praying that our God is faithful to preserve you to the finish line. In addition, let me share some simple truths for your arsenal as you fight the good fight. Most of what I will share in this section has proven very effective for me, and I believe it will also for you as you walk in the faith in this world of chaos.

All of this starts and ends with us allowing the Holy Spirit to guide and control our efforts; we can't allow ourselves to make excuses as most victims would. Giving and serving requires a commitment or action on our part. Growing is the return on investment for the effort we put into providing a service. God has designed us to be in a community with one another for fellowship, encouraging, and growing together: His Kingdom on Earth. This can only be done effectively if we are in a healthy place.

I have learned the following things in my journey to become all Christ has commissioned me to be. Case in point, I can remember working with various ministries and outreaches in serving people experiencing homelessness, generally by feeding them and providing hygiene products. This was done through snow, sleet, or rain all year round. When I first started serving in this capacity, I had no idea that God would grow and heal me through this. At first, blessing others made me feel good; I loved cooking, creating meals, and serving with other volunteers one cup of coffee at a time. But as the years went by, the church we began attending did not have a homeless outreach, and I started doing other ministries. Returning to the homeless ministry years later, it was so easy to reconnect with the people that I felt at home again. When Covid hit our city, ministries closed their doors, and God gave me the idea to start feeding those living on the streets and under bridges. It was in this season that Bridge Street Outreach was formed as a 501(c)(3). God used this to help me take my eyes off myself and be used for a greater purpose.

At the beginning of 2023, my pastor approached me and said, "This will be the year God will grant you the desire of your heart." The passion that was burning inside me was to help believers in Christ win their battle with mental struggles. In the spring of 2023, I received my Certified Mental Health Coach certification, and by the fall, a Mental Health Support Group made his word fulfilled and alive in me. God uses our experiences, trials, and tribulations to help us relate to those struggling within the same area; He uses us to become relatable to the broken and hurting. Sure, God can use anyone to counsel others, using scriptures, but sometimes it is good to hear, "Yes! I know exactly how you feel!" If I struggle with an addiction, I will find comfort and relatability with someone who has walked in my shoes—someone who can share in the struggles but also point me in a direction to help, which is what I hope to accomplish in this chapter.

Our Spiritual Walk

We talked about CBT, and I mentioned briefly the term Self-Care. Taking care of ourselves covers more than just hygiene but also includes other things like sleep, rest, diet, exercise, and spending time with God in His presence. My favorite character in the Bible, Elijah, who suffered from depression, is a great example. When Elijah was at the end of his rope, he wanted to die, but God sent an angel to feed him and give him rest (1 Kings 19:3-8). God did not beat him but ministered to him through rest and nourishment. This is the best illustration of a Father's love for his child that I can reference, and this love is more significant than any earthly father's love. I remember when God showed me the error of comparing an earthly father to Him, my Heavenly Father. There is no comparison; God's love for us is even greater than we could ever experience in this earthly realm. Our heavenly Father wants to comfort and heal us through this, restoring what was stolen from us. God wants us as we are and calls us to cast all our cares upon Him. He is not afraid of our hurts, emotions, or even our outbursts of anger. In these moments, God can use those things to reveal Himself to us.

Well, Let's Just See How the Day Goes

I remember one early morning devotion time I had with God. I was reading about Elijah and picking up on his intense emotions. I read how God showed up and helped Elijah demonstrate great power to the people of Israel. But in the next chapter, he sits under a tree, depressed and wanting to die. I asked God, "How Elijah could forget the great works that You did in his life and become so depressed and suicidal?" I heard in my spirit God say to me, "I don't know, my son; how can you be?" God has been so good and faithful to me during my life. He has proven to be good even when I am not. What was designed by the enemy for destruction, God has turned around for my good. I saw rejection, failure, and ruin for years, but God has used all of it for His purpose. I had to experience all of this for such a time to share my story. Despite all the pain, God has allowed me to help others by coaching and cheering them on. Rest in Him, and show some grace for yourself. I still have days where I question all of this and whether I am worthy. My depression challenges me, and my faith becomes weak. These moments are opportunities to use CBT skills, reading the word, and fellowship to pull us through.

If you look at my walk, like many others, you will see many peaks and valleys, but what's important to see is God's faithfulness. There were times throughout my journey that I gave up on my faith; I would make soul-wrenching remarks against the God of Heaven and Earth. I will admit that if I were God, some people would no longer exist, and lighting bolts from heaven would be a daily occurrence. My childhood taught me many negative emotions; it showed me people's faults and how people couldn't be trusted, even our caregivers. Unlike many Christians, my rose-colored glasses never existed, and I held unforgiveness towards the church. Sure, I could understand the world, but I lacked grace and was critical of everything the church represented. I expected the church to forgive my imperfections but lacked the same mercy I was expecting. That is a double standard, and God could not start His healing process in me until I repented and forgave the church. According to a profile test I took, my attachment style is a disorganized or disassociated type, which means: "I hate you; please don't leave me." This type is rooted in early childhood trauma and represents the attachment acquired from a parent or caregiver. If a parent abuses a child, a mixed message is sent that says my nurturing caregiver should be trusted but isn't. This message affects us mentally and spiritually; it made it hard for me to forgive the church, and it breaks down our ability to trust and rest in God.

How We Treat Ourselves

I bet you thought I would forget the two most unbearable subjects, diet and exercise, didn't you? Well, it is my experience that we eat our emotions and dig our holes deeper with forks. My first college degree was an Associate of Applied Science specializing in Dietetic Technology. Sound impressive? No, it is simply a two-year degree, a step below what Dietitians have. From my studies of nutrition and healthy eating, I can testify that certain types of food can and will impact your overall mood. I often attest to studies and common sense when stating proven facts and personal experiences. If you have an antique car, you want only the best to maintain it; you polish it and put only the best fuel into it to ensure ultimate performance. We are no different, especially as we age; we learn that we might not be able to eat as we did in earlier years. Studies have proven time and time again that sugar, trans fats, and certain chemicals can affect your overall health. We truly become what we eat; cheap and processed is not how I want to become. Before eating, ask yourself, "Am I really starving," or is this emotional eating?" If it is hunger, I suggest observing your feelings while making food choices. Hearing that tiny voice say, "I don't care" or "I feel like" may be a sign that the options you're about to choose might not be good ones.

We also see studies proving that exercising helps release endorphins that help you feel happy. An additional benefit to exercising is that it keeps us limber as we age. A couple of years ago, I was diagnosed with an autoimmune disease called Ankylosing Spondylitis. This condition leaves older men hunching over as the discs in the spine fuse. Doctors advised me to avoid inflammatory foods and increase my exercise routine to remain limber. In our depression, we become passive, complacent, and make bad choices. The Bible challenges us in Deuteronomy 30:19- 20 with the well-known set of options: I set before you blessings and curses—you choose! I know, once again, this passage is talking more about spiritual aspects, but the principles of choosing and the consequences are the points I am trying to make. If I choose unhealthy foods, I will reap ill feelings and emotions, and my body will probably react the same.

Under the umbrella of self-care, I want to clarify that how and what we eat is just as important as hygiene and rest. When we think of self-care, it is generally assumed that it is about outward practices that make us feel better and cared for, like a bubble bath full of bubbles. Still, we forget that our internal being can also dictate our emotional state of mind and motivation. I want to address the inner being and what I learned about when battling mental health issues. As temples of the Holy Spirit, we must do our best to become good stewards of what we have been given, even if life hasn't dealt us the best health. I am not the perfect example of what I am about to say, but I try, often succeeding, even while ailing in some areas. At one point in my life, eating my emotions led me to an all-time weight of four hundred pounds; I struggled to do life. I knew how to care for myself, but it had become a vicious cycle, a battle I could not win alone.

The idea that we are what we eat is accurate, and our choices will determine how and what we feel at any moment. While consuming a decadent dessert like a hot fudge sundae, I have never heard anyone express a desire to run a marathon or work out for an hour in the gym. Likewise, I never felt positively charged to do or think anything good after eating high sugar levels. Depression and anxiety can cause us to eat our emotions, and when we do, it is never a healthy, balanced meal—trust me. I never said, "Wow, I am so depressed; let me eat a healthy salad or a steak dinner." My selection involved sugar, processed food, and refined simple carbohydrate choices. These choices often came as quick impulses from an irrational state of mind. This was great for the fast-food industry but not for my bottom line. Simple carbohydrates are mainly man-produced and filled with bad fats and simple quick-burning sugars that are easily accessible and often affordable. As a kid, I remember dealing with depression and living in fear of my abusers, stopping into a Five and Dime store after school and buying four different candy bars for a dollar. I then walked home and consumed all of them within fifteen minutes before I got to my front door. Sure, it initially brought me instant gratification, but hours later, I would feel sick, sluggish, and tired. Even knowing the feeling, I would repeat this same scene over again when I was stressed, depressed, or in fear. This habit is hard to break, and with time, it only worsens; it affects the brain and joints and can lead to diabetes.

As I mentioned, my studies in Dietetics were my first introduction to healthy eating, and it was here that I learned most of my nutritional facts, but as you know, learning never stops. As with any medical diagnosis, I always knew that, in some small way, food was one of the culprits in how I felt, and better food could help me become healthier. I started reading and watching holistic doctors on social media outlets, and you can identify them because pharmaceutical companies do not fund them. Another disclaimer here is to weigh everything you hear, know the resources, and consider opposing views. Take what applies to you, your food preferences, and what seems reasonable; for example, cherries are my favorite fruit, which helps reduce arthritic inflammation. But if someone told me the same thing about Brussels sprouts, I would have to learn how to live with Art and his inflammation. After all, we will never stay on course if we can't embrace and follow the path. I had to listen to my body and incorporate this into the self-care applications mentioned by professionals like counselors.

Self-care is both internal and external because of such concepts as how much sleep we receive; other principles contribute to how we feel and proceed with life. My four-hundred-pound life was also courtesy of highly sugared, carbonated beverages we call pop, soda, or politically correct, soda-pop. When sugar and carbonation are introduced into our body, it is considered empty calories and causes bloating. But what if I drink diet colas? Well, let us talk about that one for a quick minute; it is now an artificial chemical with carbonation. The brain doesn't recognize the chemical, and the body does not know how to process it. So, in essence, this is even worse. My journey to lose weight was for overall health reasons, and I watched several documentaries about our food supply and case studies reflecting Western civilization diets. In these documentaries, like so many others, we see that we don't know what we don't know. In this case, ignorance is not bliss.

Respecting Ourselves and Others

Learning what things we should keep to ourselves and when, where, or how to release these things has been the most challenging lesson for me. You've heard the phrase, "Not everyone is entitled to your opinion"? I have learned that not everyone is entitled to my inner world. This is what is meant by the words, "Bigger fences make better neighbors." The more we share with others, the more confusion we cause ourselves because everyone has an opinion of how to solve things. I am not advocating isolation, burying your emotions, or even closing off from the world. But I am suggesting the idea of setting up healthy borders.

There are three realms to consider when setting up these borders. The first is called intimate; you hold it close to your chest or heart, and these are your loved ones, consisting of family and possibly your best friend(s). We also need to be honest and open to those in the area of counseling so they can get an accurate picture to make a precise diagnosis and care plan. The second range is personal, going from your chest to your elbow. This will include casual friends, co-workers, and people you interact with daily. Then we have social, going from your chest to the tip of the middle finger of your outstretched arm. These are the people that we might call acquaintances or even total strangers. Either way, you might know them because of a friend or see them once in a blue moon. These ranges reflect how much information we allow others to have on us and our internal world. Not everyone will support or understand your life and how you process things. Salt and sugar look the same from a distance but have two different tastes and textures up close. Telling our story should be selective and used to testify of God's mercy, His healing ability, and His redemptive power over sin. In making borders, we protect ourselves from most unknown daily variables. But we don't want to live paranoid and oversensitive, looking for monsters around every corner.

When we enter into relationships with others, we need to make a few calculations before we let them in and at what level. What role will they have in my life? If it may be serious or long term, are they able to be trusted? Are they people in for a reason and season, or are they there till the end? How will they respond or react to the deepest part of me? How will this affect our relationship in the long run? Can this sharing come back to haunt me? Will it improve our relationship or be used to judge me in the future? I am not offering these questions to cause you to be skeptical or jaded but rather guarded, employing wisdom and avoiding additional pain. We must ask God to reveal those faithful, lifelong friends and family to us so we can heal properly and grow in understanding who He has made us to be. He has indeed made us to be in community with one another, but it is very important to know your tribe. I will discuss the tribe and its place in recovery a little later.

Journaling and Poetry

The therapy of journaling and the ability to process your emotions that way has recently come up in several conversations for me. This might be good for some, but I can only do this sometimes, and it is more in the form of poetry. Anything that puts your thoughts and emotions into words you can read and process is good. It helps in the present and can help you process those emotions and seasons in the future. Questions surrounding how you felt, the situation, and the solution will help you develop tools and get through this season sooner. Also, consider bringing these things to your sessions if you see someone for help because words are solid, robust, and revealing. Your thoughts on paper carry weight and help illuminate things you might not see in your writings.

In one case, a person who had been raped and abused by her parents would use Daddy (innocence) and Father (authoritarian) to describe their relationship. As an adult, processing the words she used as a child helped reveal to the counselor that she was talking about the same man within the same role but used different titles when talking about the male parent in her childhood. This is a clear sign of abuse within a given connection. As we write from the heart, our subconscious is tapped into, and we can learn subtle and hidden messages. I remember writing poetry and saving it to my computer, and one day I noticed my desktop was polluted with so many poems. The thought came to me: maybe I should print these out and put them into a binder for my family, just in case I die. As they were printing, I started reading them, and like an old song playing, it took me back.

Writing a journal or poetry is like a window into our soul and a mirror reflecting outward. It helps us process as we get these emotions out on paper, and in the future, it reminds us where we've been. Like a gauge or measuring device, it helps us see how far we have come. It supports and validates where we have been and the process that has brought us to where we are today. It reminds us, lest we forget, of a testimony of who God has been in our journey and how we have allowed him to rescue and save us. Several poems I have written, like "The Cave" or "The Bridge," will enable me to take a deep breath, reflect, and exhale, remembering the pain I felt writing it back then. At this moment, I realize that maybe I am not where I should be at times within the present, but thank God I am not where I used to be. We need to remember that our life is a marathon, not a sprint, like the Apostle Paul, who ran the race and fought a good fight. We must remind ourselves as believers that God is good, and our hope must always rest with Him. My poems reflected my hurt, pain, and heart on paper and clarified what I was missing. This realization helped me seek after God in what was needed to restore me. Writing is highly recommended as a therapy method to get our emotions out so we can see them. This process acts as an activation. Reusing bottled-up feelings helps us process because we can see clearly.

Personality Profiles

Before I start talking about this subject matter, I want to be unequivocally clear. As a Christian, I believe in what the scriptures say regarding God, His son, the Holy Spirit, and who I am as His child. I am not looking at what I have discovered in my journey as a religion or a new, improved Gospel. That said, I believe God created each of us with a unique personality influenced by our culture and environment, which has become a lens through which we see and interpret situations. If you were going on a trip back in my day, you had to learn how to unfold, read, and re-fold this huge paper called a map. It was an outline of all sorts of roads and routes that helped us find our way. Sometimes, these maps changed or became updated with new roads. We change throughout life because of discoveries, changing times, and the constant flow of people entering and exiting our journey. Sometimes, the changes we encounter are subtle, or they can be immense because of unexpected events. Unexpected life events can affect us mentally and emotionally, resulting in trauma. Like the map, it is a new entrance or exit ramp we needed a reference to, making the old map obsolete. These changes can also alter our personalities.

God created us with a core character, and then life comes with all its experiences and somehow forms us. These events change how we view life within our social environment; they mark how we see and respond to triggers. Elijah experienced God's mighty moves, yet one threat from an evil queen triggered him, and his reaction was isolation in a cave. Elijah

Well, Let's Just See How the Day Goes

suffered from depression, and his nature was to walk alone and internalize. He didn't need a following and often questioned his ability to represent God. I am guessing from what we know from 1 Kings that Elijah was probably an Introverted, Intuitive, Feeling, and Judging (I.N.F.J); according to the Myers Briggs 16 personality profile, and this is the rarest of all sixteen types. Was he always an INFJ? Did Elijah experience a life-changing event that made him like this?

In my world, people can only be trusted once they have proven themselves; as a guarded person, I determine what and how I share with others. But that wasn't always the case when I was younger, inexperienced, and just wanting to be liked was my goal. I felt everyone needed to know everything about me. As I have grown and learned valuable lessons, I am learning less is more, and others might not know how to take my story. What message is being sent, how others might process the information, and most importantly, how they can use it against me, has become so important. As I mentioned, a narrative will be told, but how accurate? There is a saying, "It's best to remain quiet and be thought a fool than to speak and remove all doubt." I know what you're probably thinking; this sounds hard or bitter, leading to isolation or not being accountable to others. On the contrary, we need fellowship with others, but most importantly, we need it with God first.

This reminds me of an old Hymn we used to sing, "What a Friend We have in Jesus." Part of the lyrics went: Have we trials and temptations, Are there troubles everywhere? Do thy friends despise and forsake thee? ... Jesus knows our every weakness, all because we do not carry everything to God in prayer. We tell everyone our deepest and darkest secrets, replacing the one that can heal and restore us. Most things we tell others only help us discredit our Heavenly Father's majestic faithfulness and power within our lives. We use people as sounding boards and believe they can help us solve everything. I am unsure that was God's initial plan with Adam in the garden. Sure, fellowship, mentoring, and counseling are in our daily lives, but their intensity and frequency must be balanced.

Knowing who we are and how we respond, interact, and process information is crucial in recovery and in understanding who we are in Christ. Have you ever had unexplained medical symptoms and experienced frustration over not having a diagnosis? Then, when there was a diagnosis, how relieved you must have felt, no matter how serious the condition. Even if it is severe, when the doctor says, "Here is how we will address this condition," a care plan is made. When my wife Lynda and I married in 1991, the people we hung out with thought they knew us. I was the life of the party, working hard to entertain and engage with others; Lynda was quiet, always observing. When we hosted parties, she would talk to a few people, as I was the biblical Martha. My perceived duty was to make everyone feel included, engaged, and having fun. If you asked everyone who knew us, I was the extrovert, and my wife was the introvert. But years of research, including both of us taking these personality tests, has shown us something different. The classic sign of an introvert is how groups of people make us feel. If social gatherings drain you, or you prefer a quiet evening over having company, you, my friend, might be an introvert. You feel drained after guests leave and desperately need downtime to decompress; you, my friend, are indeed an introvert. And it turns out, that is me too. When you are diagnosed with severe depression, others will accuse you of isolating and avoiding others when the actual reason is your need to decompress. This may be the most important topic you will get out of this book; I can't express it enough. So, I encourage you to take a few personality tests and get the long overdue diagnosis you need to start your care plan. Use this information as a map, knowing we change and continue to change; be careful not to use it as a religion. Don't pigeonhole yourself with word curses like, "I am always like this" or "This is just how I am;" this is not meant to be a death sentence.

When I found out that my personality was aligned with the characteristics of the Myers Briggs INFJ, or even the Enneagram 4 (Individualist), I didn't broadcast it on the rooftops. Still, it did help me understand and articulate myself to others. When you learn about yourself through these tests, understand that not one test can pinpoint you 100%, meaning you might not identify and agree with everything it says. The Enneagram test shows your main trait, but then it tells you how you might act when you are not in a healthy frame of mind and how it differs from when you are healthy. As an Individualist, I can be a Helper (2) when my depression is low and I am in harmony. When I am unhealthy, focusing on my depression, I become a Perfectionist (1) and very judgmental. This information I have learned about myself acts as my map, showing me how to navigate because of what I have learned from these profiles. Knowing my personality can help me predict how I might respond to certain conditions, allowing me to change any negative responses.

Since discovering my Myers Briggs type, I have watched many psychology videos about my unique style. I must be honest; my first impression wasn't positive. My thought was, why did God make me like this? This personality type, being rare, made me feel weird and like an outcast or socially inept. Interestingly enough, in further researching my kind, I discovered others like me that you may have heard about. The following people throughout history, like me, were INFJs: Martin Luther King Jr., Mother Teresa, Mahatma Gandhi, Princess Dianna, and Nelson Mandela. When I think about it, I am in good company. The INFJ types are defined as creative, passionate, dedicated, and, as you can see, fighters against social injustice. I also saw something in writing that implied Jesus may have been an INFJ. Based on what I know about myself and what I have read about Jesus, teaching to the crowds exhausted him. he had compassion and desired to heal, but most importantly, he needed time alone with His Father.

Knowing your Tribe

As I mentioned earlier, I wasn't able to walk through recovery alone, and I needed what is called a support group. My support group consisted of my immediate family members and pastor, those I would have considered Pro-Rick! So that we are clear, out of my children, only my eldest and only son was on it—not that my three daughters weren't pro-dad, but he was the only one not looking at it personally. He didn't try to figure out why I wanted to die, but he remained focused on how I needed to avoid or redirect those feelings. He was relentlessly questioning the new meds I was taking and treatments I was prescribed. He also was a strong support for his mother. My daughters loved me but couldn't get past the suicide ideation leading to my attempts; they just loved me and knew they didn't want to lose me. My sister was my prayer warrior, using our childhood experiences to rationalize my feelings.

That made up my internal family circle, but what do you do when triggers come from within your family? Beyond doctors and counselors, everyone should have at least one or two external supports. My external support consisted of a long-time friend, Curt, who may not have understood my internal struggles, but because we met within the workplace, he knew when and how I would become triggered at work. Being a man of faith, Curt would always encourage and challenge me, constantly referencing scripture and the attributes of God. Curt was the older brother I never had, always pointing me to Christ, checking up on me, and challenging the believer within me.

I was also incredibly blessed to have sessions with my pastor, who had medical insight because his wife was a nurse. In an early session with him, I confided in a new negative behavior I was experiencing, and he asked me for a list of medications. He saw the drugs and pointed out one with similar side effects to what I was experiencing. He walked me through my childhood trauma and defined my mother's condition and parenting style. Through my sessions with him, he helped peel back the veil that blinded me and helped me mentally and spiritually understand what I was experiencing. Every Christian needs a strong, spiritually filled mentor and pastor to guide them through personal trauma. In this setting, truth is spoken, and natural healing can take shape. I also suggest another layer of seeking additional support through a trained and certified counselor.

My tribe was there, sowing into me what I needed and equipping me with the tools to become who I am today. I will be eternally grateful for their love, support, and patience. As Elijah rested and was fed and cared for by an angel, God ministered to him in nourishment and rest; through that season, Elijah regained the strength he needed. But in the end, Elijah moved on, restored and ready to minister; the angels no longer fed him. The scenery changed as I started to walk out my recovery, healing and growing strong in my faith and emotional health.

Those who helped me in crisis mode changed as I recovered, which is normal. My wife remained my wife, but her role as the caregiver in keeping me safe from myself changed. My pastor went from providing crisis intervention and counseling sessions to regular Sunday morning meetings. I viewed my journey as moving from the ER in crisis mode to rehab, learning to walk again. I am not encouraging removing friends and family from your life once you are in a better place. But in recovery, we are different from who we were in crisis, so the support group often changes or becomes less involved. Sometimes, removing people from your new season is crucial if they remind you of your trauma or treat you as if you are still in crisis.

Sometimes, you must remind others, "That was then, and this is now" and remind them that your past is not a life sentence. But it would be best to assure them that you will be open and honest with them when things aren't going well. Your family and friends love you and want you to be in a safe place, and if they were there in the struggles, they need to be assured from time to time that you are okay now.

Counseling versus Coaching

In addition to having a personalized support group of the ones who know you best, it never hurts to receive professional help. As I mentioned, I am a Certified Christian Mental Health Coach. You're probably wondering what that is and how it differs from straight counseling. If you have any experience with counseling, you know that they deal primarily with your present condition by referencing your past. For example, if you struggle with anxiety, they would be able to tie that to something from earlier childhood. This is good because it helps you know your condition and why you are experiencing the symptoms associated with your anxiety. But now that you have been made aware of this condition and possible triggers, what will you do with it? How can you manage and work through it now or in the future? Anxiety is often brought on when we are unaware of something happening or about to happen. It is accompanied by symptoms one would experience when fleeing a bear chasing you. Unless you are in the woods or zoo, this fear is unwarranted, but in your current setting, your brain can perceive it as accurate. At this point, knowing why I feel this way because of past trauma, I need to know how to reduce the anxiety and deal with my current reality.

This is where the coaching comes in and helps you in the present situation. Think of a sports coach or the new onset of "Life Coaches." You are in a game, and the goal is to win. However, to win, you need practice, strength training, and insight into the best moves to make for that win. I read a phrase once: "Life is like looking both ways before crossing the street just to get hit by an airplane." How true is that? As you can imagine, our lives can change unexpectedly without notice. We live in a fast-paced world with constant stimulation and an off button that can be hard to find. Coaching reminds us of this; just like in sports, plays are rehearsed. The coach presents potential scenarios and opposing moves to throw you off your game. The boxing coach might show you how to duck and weave to avoid that heavy blow. As with all coaches, we want you to succeed, live successfully, and master the art of survival.

The best news is that, unlike counseling, which can go on for years, coaching is meant to be accomplished in short and time-certain intervals. When someone comes in for help to overcome grief over the loss of a loved one, the goal is to help the person through it, identifying the feelings and how they can be reduced, and the person can then continue as they recover and integrate into a new normal. But we all know that overcoming grief is a process that may take a lifetime. Coaching isn't curing distress and abandoning the loss as if it never happened but moving on through it. Acknowledging the loss of my cousin when he died, it took me almost a year to come to terms with the state of his salvation alone. During that time, I wasn't sure if he made it right and accepted Christ, even as he lay unconscious on his deathbed. The first stage of grief wasn't just him being absent from my life but where he would spend eternity. The cause of suffering isn't always a loss of life; many aspects tie into grief.

Counseling sessions will illuminate the causes and how we view the emotions we experience. It will tell us how to manage them until the next session, but coaching supplements these sessions with accountability. Counseling told me what to do, but I was alone throughout my days between sessions. I had a set of orders, but I lacked the skills to employ them, and if I got hit by an airplane, now what? Coaching is short-term; after you learn what muscle needs to be strengthened, the next step is enhancing it and remembering the importance of keeping up the exercise. Counseling tells us which muscle; coaching tells us how and when to strengthen ourselves for the win! When battling depression, anxiety, or any other mental health condition, we must remember that it may take various approaches or techniques to overcome. We are not all alike; our symptoms and how we arrive at our healing will depend on multiple factors. These factors may be our spiritual condition, how we manage triggers, and what we can relate to throughout the process. When I started my journey to recovery, I will admit my spiritual man was almost dead, and my faith was on life support. I wanted to die! While I was in the hospital, other patients were constantly causing me to trigger and respond out of fear and anger. When introduced to therapy techniques, I was reluctant and dismissive of their ability to cure this brokenness. Counseling was my first step; coaching has helped me live with and through my in-between sessions with applications I must use on this road of recovery.

Addressing Depression

I wrote this book as a memoir of my life, faith, and things I have incorporated into healing myself. I would like you to consider this revelation I have had and see if it is something that might change your life. We often say, "I deal with depression." Another word for "deal" is cope, which leads us to believe that we must effectively work with it, survive, and shift around this depression. It sounds like much work and can become draining when things need to get done. In the previous chapter, I told you about how to employ Cognitive Behavioral Therapy to manage the effects of depression. Managing depression is for some, and was at one point in my life, a full-time, seven-days-a-week task. I used to refer to myself as a "highly functioning depressant." Well, here is the revelation I would like to present for your consideration. Instead of dealing with depression, what would it look like if we learned how to "partner" with it, replacing coping with the emphasis on working with depression and accomplishing great things? In partnering, the word "part" is right there, suggesting making something part of something else. In other words, we won't live under and become subjected to it, but in the presence of depression, we will make it just another part of us used to do something good. In depressive states, we focus on ourselves and our internal world; it's about me and no one else. When I found myself partnering with my depression were those times when I could become creative and make words take on life through my writings. Later, I will share with you a couple of these writings. I became more creative when I said, "I am depressed, but I will find ways to serve others." Partnering is saying, "I will bring depression into my current situation and find ways to make it work well in and through my abilities and talents."

Please hear me out: I am not suggesting that we agree on the impact depression has in our lives. Instead, I'm talking about commanding it to stay in its place. I am sure you have heard the phrase, "Do it Afraid," and I am saying the same thing here. To give it a mental image, I would say to myself, "I am driving and depressed. Depression, if you have to come along, take the back seat." There were many times I would show up to a commitment with an internal struggle, but in keeping my word, I had to employ this mindset. I will also attest that during these times, I used extra effort, and with passion fueling me, my performance was better than I would have typically done.

The Bible contains examples of God calling zeros and turning them into heroes. We make ourselves the zeros because of how we see ourselves, and then we project that onto others and our Heavenly Father. The good news is that our opinions die in the presence of the Father of all truth. Gideon was a great example of this, but God called him a mighty man of valor (Judges 6:12). This simple man living in fear, probably oppressed and depressed, had been associated with and labeled the weakest, yet God saw something different. I would often stand amazed at how God used me in my depression for others. I remember one time in church with my wife. I was depressed and wanted to leave, but my wife leaned over and said, "You have a word of encouragement for this person in front of us." I didn't think I was in the right mindset, yet the words I gave brought healing to that person. God never calls the qualified; He qualifies the ones that He calls. The notion that we deal with depression is partly bondage, but partnering is coexisting and using it for something good, creative, and beneficial. I want to encourage you with this: allow God to define you within your brokenness, letting Him heal and restore you to His ultimate design for your life. God had our story written before the foundations of the world. The enemy will try to destroy it; we have to choose to allow the author to write it out.

My disclaimer is that I am not exempting the need in some cases for medication, medical advice, or other complex medical treatments; after all, I have been there. I have trusted almost every medical intervention I was initially presented with. My pastor and his medical knowledge helped me question and become an advocate for myself. This was a turning point in my life, changing how I viewed the term doctors use in their quest to "Practice Medicine." After researching, reading, and learning new concepts, I gained control and was able to make decisions I felt were right for me. Just like our spiritual walk with Christ, we are unique. I asked God to heal or kill, and, as always, God chooses life, which is abundantly rich and full of mercy and grace. We need to accept that and lean into these promises because we know this battle and all the others are never-ending on this side of Heaven. In my struggle with Major Depression Disorder, I have learned so far that depression enslaved me to focus inward; I found my escape in serving and helping others and creatively writing out these emotions. Partnering doesn't dismiss depression; instead of getting lost within yourself, work with and despite it. Allow God to use you in the midst of it and start your day with the statement, "Let's Just See How the Day Goes."

Depression, grief, and other mental health conditions can be summed up as Spiritual Battle. We are trying to regain control and continue in the fight, so we need to address the type of warfare and dismantle its power in our lives. This can be accomplished in several ways. First, we need to address what is lacking and our real needs. I needed to replace my oppressive feelings with a heavy garment of praise in worship. This was completed every time I actively chose to put on worship music and turn my heart and eyes toward God in heaven. Isaiah chapter sixty-one tells us how and why we need this in our walk and what the results will be. It is a proven fact that music affects our lives, and the genre we choose can produce good or bad outcomes. Worship music can also redirect our thoughts from ourselves to the one who can set us free. Another consideration is reading encouraging scriptures from the Bible or stories of God's miraculous power in overcoming some of the impossible situations saints encountered. For example, Job's challenge to God and God's reply found in Job thirty-eight and thirty-nine assure us that God knows, sees, and can deliver us from every vain imagination. So reading and worshiping is a gift from God to be used both corporately in church and privately throughout the week to edify and build us up. Both corporate and individual worship and reading can and should be done throughout the week and not limited to one or two days a week. If you are not currently doing this, you are missing the cornerstone of your faith and the steps needed to grow your Spiritual life.

Suicide and Suicidal Ideation

After moving to Cleveland at fifteen, I wondered who I was after years of fear, abuse, and near-death experiences. For the first time, I was in a safe place, cared for by my mother's oldest sister. My aunt, a survivor herself, never believed in physically disciplining her son, and I benefited from her parenting style. However, by age eighteen, something was missing; no one needed me or demanded anything from me. I went from receiving negative attention to none at all. Even when I acted out in anger, I was only verbally corrected. I was updated with positive reinforcement and redirected with words when I broke something or did something terrible. This was a cultural shock; I did not know how to handle this parenting style. I got to a point where I missed the attention; even if it had been violent abuse or any other form of attention, it was no longer present. When this lifestyle is the only point of reference you have ever known, this change can affect you.

Around this time, I started drinking with my cousin and school friends and experimenting with amphetamines and marijuana. In the fall of 1989, after a couple of disappointments and a break-up, I decided maybe life wasn't all that great. After writing my first suicide letter ever, and with eyes full of tears, I took an entire bottle of sleeping pills. A friend called me and asked if he could come over, and according to him, I sounded unusual and avoided his question. I next remember being in a hospital Emergency Room with tubes down my throat and watching the pills floating out of my body. In recovery, it was reported to me that I was found lifeless on my couch, with a Bible clutched to my chest. I wanted to die, and I believed God would understand why and hoped He would accept me. It was here that I realized I needed my Heavenly Father more than the life He gave me. I was clinically diagnosed with Major Depression Disorder and spent three weeks in a lockdown unit.

My attempts did not stop there; as the years went by, the thought of growing old was overshadowed by the goal of being dead by age thirty. I lived hard and fast, never considering that maybe someday God would even be able to use me. Then, in 2015, I lost a good job and struggled with the mental abuse I received from an overbearing female boss. This boss consistently hit every button and created massive triggers for me; everyone feared her. After losing my job, I started isolating and losing the desire to engage with my wife and children; my pastors' calls went unanswered. Then the day came: my wife was at work, my kids were in school, and voices from my past came back to haunt me. These voices assured me that life would be better without me; my family wouldn't be hurt. The suicidal ideations started with shame, guilt, and loathing of my existence, and the voices got louder. The enemy is compelling, and he mixes thoughts with half-truths. I started grabbing every pill I could find and dumping it before me. I called the church, desperately crying over the voices shouting and fearing I couldn't do it this time. This was the first time my pastor saw me in this condition—he was at my door the next thing I knew. Following up with inpatient services, I was diagnosed with major depression and PTSD. I know it isn't officially approved in the DSM-5. Still, my PTSD is classified as Complex PTSD because it was from multiple chronic and prolonged experiences, not from a single episode like military or sudden onsets.

After my second visit to the hospital, the unit doctor could not understand why I was on eight prescriptions ranging from depression, bipolar, and mood stabilizers; during the three weeks of inpatient treatment, he slowly weaned me off all but one medication. While in the hospital, I received two weeks of ECT, Electroconvulsive Therapy, which was intense, but the treatments were successful. This is meant for chronic depression, and it involved putting me out, wiring my head, and using voltage shock waves. I remember coming to, and every muscle in my body hurt, there were bite marks on my tongue and inner mouth, and I had a significant headache. It was intense, but it helped me on the road to recovery.

Remember, just like depression, suicidal ideation is inward-focused; you can't imagine taking one more step, let alone one more day. You can't see the light of day for the clouds; all you can see is despair. It is a permanent solution to a temporary problem. This act is final; unless caught in time, there is no undoing it. In my ideations, I wasn't even thinking how my family would feel or go on without me. I knew my family loved me, but somehow, deep down inside, I wasn't sure why. My mind could not process reality from emotions or truth from lies. My major depression and PTSD diagnosis required intensive treatments, and I stand here attesting to the impact all these treatments had on me. I remember being told that I had treatment-resistant depression and that my medication would have to change as my body got used to it constantly. This was no way for me to live, and as my medications would change, so would the side effects. Many medicines used for depression come with a warning of the potential side effect of suicidal thoughts, and I was there many times. Looking back, the two medical interventions that helped me more than medications were ECT and learning CBT coping skills. If you are someone who is taking anti-depression drugs and you are still having depression and deeper emotional issues, please re-evaluate and seek doctors who are willing to try non-medication treatments.

Invite the Comforter

One of our greatest gifts as modern-day Christians is what Jesus promised us in John 14:16-30: "I will not leave you; I will send the Holy Spirit, the Comforter, to live in you, and He will lead and comfort you." This gift wasn't entirely made available to the Old Testament believers because Jesus had not yet died and made that exchange for His church. This knowledge is by far the most helpful for who I am today. When I realized that I could use meditation and consciously allow the Holy Spirit to minister truth to me, my recovery was almost instant.

One of the pitfalls of a PTSD mind is misinterpreting social and interpersonal cues. I would get offended when someone acted a certain way, and my emotions would overreact, and a snap judgment and rejection would set off triggers. My first defense would be to pull away and cut off all communication. Treating people like this was a strategy from my childhood, and it was centered on shame; the idea would be that I would reject you before you rejected me. In other words, if someone were leaving this relationship first, it would be me. I remember being exhausted from treating or reacting to people like this, especially those close to me. This would lead me to withdraw and build walls to protect myself from things I conjured up in my mind. This behavior would only confuse my family and friends and lead me deeper into my shame. Then, one day, with my eyes filled with tears, I remember praying, "God, heal me or kill me; I can't keep going on like this!" I felt this peace coming over me, like a warm blanket, and I felt an unconditional love and a voice saying, "I will; let me!" We serve a God who loves us so much, but He respects us enough to heal us not through force but by our own will.

As I walk through this life and come across these triggers now, they don't sting as much, and I attribute that to the way I ask the Holy Spirit to lead and guide me in the truth. When I was processing the cues wrong, it was because I wasn't processing the facts but my perceived reality. Now, I ask the Holy Spirit to show me and help me see with the eyes of Christ what is true. When we walk in His truth, we also experience His peace, producing hope. So, the next time you feel angry, depressed, anxious, or hopeless, invite the Comforter into those emotions. Ask the Holy Spirit to illuminate His light on those dark areas and reveal the truth. When this happens, you will also feel a gentle nudge to forgive or repent of whatever is at the root cause of those feelings. This would happen to me many times, where something that I did or someone did to me would become recessed in my mind, and the Holy Spirit would have to remind me. Remember the nature of God according to Romans 8:1: "Therefore, there is no condemnation to those in Christ, who walk not after the flesh but dwell within the Spirit." When the Holy Spirit points out something, causing us to remember, it is gentle, not condemning, leading us to surrender and repentance.

These are the things that I have learned in my recovery. The process wasn't easy at times, but in the long run, it all worked out. I am not saying that I'm healed and no longer need to activate these methods occasionally. I am saying that when I struggle, I remember the importance and how to employ these strategies. We need to understand that mental and emotional struggles come from various places. Like me, some people have struggled from an abusive childhood; others may attribute theirs to chemical imbalances. Whatever the cause, we can become victorious. My most impactful resource is learning and accepting who I am in Christ beyond the broken little boy. I went from being an abused victim to a warrior in an ongoing battle to help others. The struggle isn't over, but God gave me weapons within my arsenal to become stronger and an overcomer.

So far, I have shown you things I have done for myself internally that helped me heal and recover. When the enemy tries to label me as a victim, God reminds me that He sees me differently. The Bible instructs us to take these and other corrupt thoughts into captivity according to 2 Corinthians 10:5, and I want you to know this is imperative for those of us who can get lost within our minds. Keeping our thoughts in check keeps us from wandering away from God's truth. Being in our right mind helps us see God as a loving Father, helps us interpret situations within our world, and helps us become less offended around those who do love and care for us.

When we learn these steps, we are on the road to healing and becoming what God has created us to be. I realized that even though it wasn't God's plan for me to suffer, He would use it for His glory and purpose.

As a Christian Mental Health Coach, I can relate with, understand, and be sympathetic to those God gives me. I can sit in the darkness of depression and help you identify the triggers because I was once there, too. Because of my experience, I can allow God to help illuminate how He can heal you and turn your story into triumph. The map I discussed can help you with your destination and bring you to a place of hope and safety. Remember, the enemy wants you to think you are the only one, but that is the biggest lie ever told. He will use it to keep you from others if you believe it. It's not the beginning that matters but how we finish. Allow God to heal you in His way, using these tools and allowing others to partner with you on this life-changing voyage.

Forgiveness

I almost forgot the most liberating and healing part of my journey, besides my faith in Christ and allowing God to heal all my broken pieces. Forgiveness is the second most significant secret ingredient to my healing and finding strength and purpose. I am sure you've heard some of this before, but it's worth reminding you that unforgiveness toward someone else is like drinking poison and hoping the other person dies. The death that keeps on killing is not forgiving, and eventually, you will be a dead man walking. I had to learn that forgiveness doesn't mean it never happened or didn't hurt but that it did, and forgiving has given me the inner peace I need. By the time I came to terms with that, my abusers were all dead, dying without saying they were sorry. For years, the thought of them dying and potentially making it right with God before doing so had infuriated me. Unforgiveness leads to anger and resentment. It torments our souls, it makes us do crazy things, and we miss out on so much living and loving others. Strong and mighty walls are built to help keep everyone else from hurting us now and potentially in the future.

I remember a little over a year after my mom passed, my sister and I met at her grave, where I had written a forgiveness letter. In this letter was something that the Holy Spirit had given me, and as I spoke the words over her grave, I cried like a baby and finally allowed my healing to take its home within me. In my letter, I acknowledged that she could only love and care for me from what she had learned and allowed God to do in her. My final sentence was that I wanted to forgive her and everyone else because I was shown grace where I had been ignored. The realization that my abusers could no longer hurt me and, like me, must someday give an account for what we have done was my deliverance. After reading this letter, I tore it up and released it into the wind. A heavy weight was lifted that day, and my eyes were finally opened. Now, when I look back, there is a sadness that I didn't forgive her while she lived. The pain of my childhood doesn't have that bitter sting anymore like it did. My mind isn't fixated on how I was treated, but now I focus on how I treat others.

Forgiveness restores our focus and puts us on a path where God can work with us to help others. God can work with damaged goods, but when He does, we change. In this change, forgiveness is inevitable and in our interest. God cannot continue His work in us without changing our hearts, and the more we resist this healing, the more complex things get and the longer we remain broken. Unlike the enemy, God comes to heal and restore us, making us in His Son's image. Jesus forgave those who put Him on the cross, those who rejected and wanted Him crucified. I must do the same daily, as God has forgiven me. It isn't easy sometimes, but God rewards us with peace when we walk in it. Also, medical studies have shown the health benefits of forgiving others because unforgiveness takes its toll on the body, mind, and spirit.

Unforgiveness is like a gateway drug. If consumed too much, it can lead to bitterness. When we hold onto unforgiveness, the roots go deep; for me, it manifested into bitterness. Then, I noticed the bitterness turning into resentment toward everyone. Resentment led me to blame others for all the emotions I was carrying within me. Blaming became my way of transferring what was in my heart to others; people never knew why I was acting this way toward them. It worsens when we blame innocent people or God for our hurt and the original sin of unforgiveness. It all starts small, a little unforgiveness; then, like a snowball rolling down a hill, it grows and becomes dangerous. We blame others or God for where we are and the offenses we have experienced instead of taking ownership of our actions, and this can be fatal. I was there, trust me; it was like spiritual cancer that kept growing and consuming innocent friends and family. Everyone became my potential enemy, and I looked around for the exit. The casualties were piling up as I crossed off names from my mental list, who would be the next ones to fall off.

Well, Let's Just See How the Day Goes

At one point, I blamed God for my pain, rejection, and abuse, which seems to be a common practice. This is the biggest lie the enemy deceives us with: he wants you to blame God, who loves you and sent His son to die for you. God hates sin, and when it entered into His creation, it broke His heart, but God gave us free will. Adam and Eve fell into sin, and we struggle with its consequences. We live in a fallen world that man corrupted, and since then humanity has paid for it, but make no mistake, one day God will bring forth justice. I had to forgive, take responsibility, stop blaming others, and allow God to repurpose my life to His plan. Today, I walk towards healing, which is new for me; when I get upset and argue with others, I step back and ask God to show me in my heart where I was wrong. When I notice a hint of bitterness or resentment, I ask God to step in and show me the root so He can remove it.

Ramblings of a Homeless Soul

As promised, I want to leave you with some of my writings that I keep in a binder called "Ramblings of a Homeless Soul." My book of poems is filled with dark days and moments of healing breakthroughs. I have learned that all these days made me who I am today. I knew in my writing how to sit with my depression and grief and not be afraid of its existence. This is where I learned to partner with these emotions and realize that I needed to move on despite them. Fellow Christians often rebuked this notion, dismissing it as not trusting Christ and not walking in a utopian world. I am here to testify that, like He did with Elijah, God met me where I was. He gave me what I needed, like a good Father would. God sat with me in my darkest times, even in the hospitals, without shame or scolding me. He loved all my broken pieces back together again and showed me the purpose of my life.

Today, I bought a pair of boxing gloves

Today, I bought a pair of boxing gloves
For a match, I did not choose
A battle I may not win
The one I cannot afford to lose
Today, I bought a pair of boxing gloves
Ones that I must put on
An unknown fight
Against an opponent, I do not see
It is a boxing ring with no ropes, only walls from within
Today, I bought a pair of boxing gloves
With one hand, I must guard, the other to throw a swing
To a voice, a thought, or maybe a reaction
I can't seem to control
Today, I bought a pair of boxing gloves
To remind me that today, I am not alone
It will be the loved ones that surround me
It will be the presence that guides me
For it will be that voice that reminds me
Of the Referee, He is in my corner and has already declared me the Winner.

Where Am I - In Your Story

Oh God, your word is filled with many rich stories
of how You worked through us, mere humans.
But it is now I struggle to see my place in Your story.
Am I a significant character?
Am I an eccentric man living off a voice or vision,
being ridiculed while building a boat?
Maybe a man tending sheep, stuttering at Your call
to deliver a captive people.
A man too old and beyond birthing a son, let
alone a nation.
One sat under a broom tree, decompressing from a
mighty victory while doubting his calling.
Or am I a small part of Your story, like a behind-the-
scenes type?
Maybe a harlot who opened up the window of her
soul for Your people.
A rebel stirred up like Jehu, fighting injustice driven
to end the reign of an evil queen.
A straightforward man, the one You labeled as a
man of valor, tasked with screening an army of men.
Regardless of his label, a man named after pain,
Jabez pleads for a larger territory, and You hear him.
But what if You called me for a new type of story

A man of deep emotions swinging like a pendulum, able to listen and relate with the broken.
One that has sat in dark places and can lead others through with light.
Maybe a simple man is willing to be used in insignificant and mundane tasks
to further Your gospel. To do justice, love mercy, and, most importantly, walk humbly with You.

My Gratitude

In my darkest night, You have been my light
In my greatest battle, You have been my refuge
When I find myself lost, You have guided me home
In all the noise, You have been my silence
When my spirit has been in a rage, You have
ordered the calm
You have taken all the wrong and somehow
made it right
An orphan spirit, You have shown me Your
Father's heart
In my homeless heart, You have been my provision
You have redeemed the time and events that were
made to destroy me and used them to help others.
I am fearfully and wonderfully made for
Your design
Mold this clay as a valuable and willing vessel
I have been through the fire, but You have been
there with me, making me who and what You desire.
Even if I make my bed in hell or soar to the ends….
even there, You will find me and bring me back.
An author known, loved, and has belonged in his
Father's arms

About the Author

Rick Rodgers is a person who has walked through severe depression, complex PTSD, and suicidal ideation and attempts. Today, he is walking out his healing as a Certified Christian Mental Health Coach and Certified Christian Life Coach. He operates a nonprofit outreach in Cleveland, Ohio, called L.I.F.T. (Loving Individuals Forming Transformations), which feeds shelter-resistant homeless people living on the streets and under bridges within the inner city. As a part of this effort, he has also formed a mental health ministry called Restoring Broken Vessels. His ministry is aimed at two primary goals: helping Christians overcome mental, emotional, and grief struggles while equipping the church with ministry support and training. Rick's ability to work and partner with all kinds of individuals and teams makes him a valuable resource in helping direct effective change within the Christian community.

Milton Keynes UK
Ingram Content Group UK Ltd.
UKHW030252190324
439698UK00015B/1027